What's it Like to Live in ...?

Canada

By Catherine Little

WATERBIRD BOOKS
Columbus, Ohio

Other Titles in This Series:

France   Italy   Jamaica

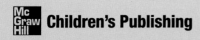

Children's Publishing

This edition published in the United States of America in 2003 by
Waterbird Books
an imprint of McGraw-Hill Children's Publishing,
a Division of The McGraw-Hill Companies
8787 Orion Place
Columbus, Ohio 43240-4027

www.MHkids.com

Library of Congress Cataloging-in-Publication Data is on file with the publisher.

© Hodder Wayland 2003

Hodder Wayland is an imprint of Hodder Children's Books

Printed in China.

1-57768-878-3

1 2 3 4 5 6 7 8 9 10 HOD 09 08 07 06 05 04 03

Contents

Where Is Canada?   4

Cities   6

The Landscape   8

The Weather   10

Transportation   12

Farming   14

Food   16

Shopping   18

Houses and Homes   20

At Work   22

Having Fun   24

Festivals   26

Canadian Scrapbook   28

Glossary   30

Further Information   31

Index   32

Where Is Canada?

Canada is a country in North America. It is a large country bordered by the United States and the Artic and Atlantic Oceans. Ottawa is Canada's capital city.

Canada is known for its cold winters and beautiful scenery.

About 30 million people live in Canada. Millions more visit the country every year.

Canada's place in the world

ARCTIC OCEAN

N
W E
S

0   500 kilometers

0   500 miles

CANADA FACTS

Canada is the second largest country in the world after Russia.

The border between Canada and the U.S.A. is about 5,592 miles long.

Huron-Iroquois Indians named the country *Canada,* which means "village" or "settlement" in their native language.

GREENLAND

Beaufort Sea

Victoria Island

Baffin Island

USA (Alaska)

Red

Mackenzie

Great Bear

Mackenzie

CANADA

Mackenzie Mountains

Yellowknife

Great Slave

Hudson Bay

● Whitehorse

Lake Athabasca

Rocky Mountains

Coast Mountains

● Edmonton

Lake Winnipeg

Vancouver

Regina

● Winnipeg

Quebec City

Newfoundland

Vancouver Island

Victoria

St Lawrence

Charlottetown

Ottawa

St John's

Montreal

USA

Toronto

The Great Lakes

Halifax

Prince Edward Island

PACIFIC OCEAN

ATLANTIC OCEAN

5

Cities

Most of Canada's cities are located in the south of the country, where it is warmer. The largest cities are Toronto, Montreal, Vancouver, and Ottawa. Fewer people live in cold northern cities like Whitehorse or Yellowknife.

Almost five million people live in Toronto.

Canada has two **official languages**, English and French. Many people speak both languages.

Canada is home to people of many different cultures.

The Landscape

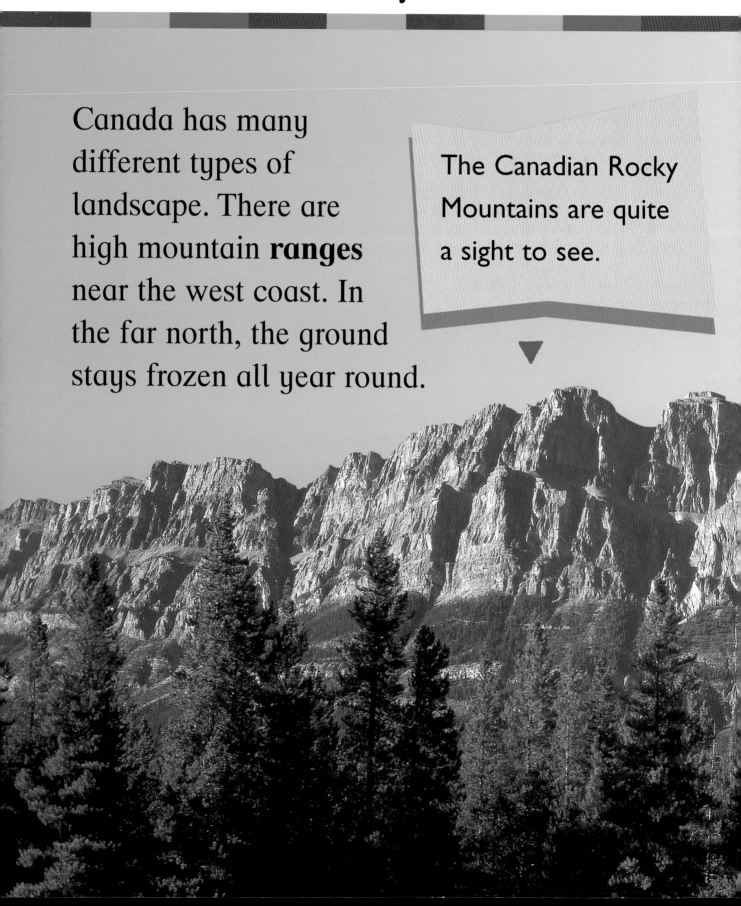

Canada has many different types of landscape. There are high mountain **ranges** near the west coast. In the far north, the ground stays frozen all year round.

The Canadian Rocky Mountains are quite a sight to see.

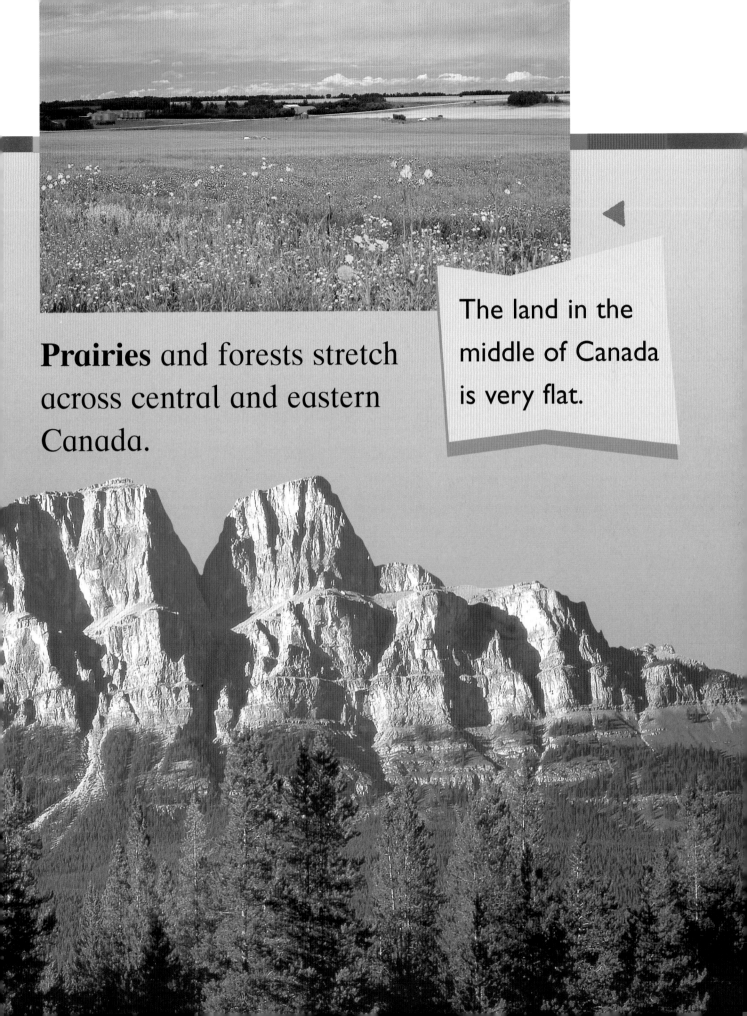

Prairies and forests stretch across central and eastern Canada.

The land in the middle of Canada is very flat.

The Weather

In Vancouver, the summers can be warm and pleasant.

The west coast of Canada has cool winters and hot summers. Eastern Canada has colder weather with icy winters and warm summers.

In northern Canada, snowdrifts are common.

In the far north, temperatures can be very low. Winters are extremely cold and snowy. Summers are usually a little warmer.

Transportation

The Trans-Canada Highway runs right across the country.

◀

People travel in Canada by airplane, train, car, and bus. The country is so large that it takes five days to drive nonstop from the east side to the west side.

In cities, people travel by bus, cable car, or underground train. The **public transportation** system is so good in Canada that people use it often and leave their cars at home.

When it is snowy, snowmobiles are a popular way to travel.

Farming

In Canada, farms can be very large. Farmers use machinery to produce big crops, such as wheat, fruit, and vegetables.

The flat **prairies** in the middle of Canada are good for growing wheat.

Canada is one of the world's largest producers of **canola**, a plant used to make oil. The word *canola* comes from the words "Canadian" and "oil."

Golden-yellow fields of canola are seen along many highways.

Food

When the weather is warm, picnics are popular.

People come from many different countries to live in Canada. That is why there are restaurants that serve food from all over the world.

In Canada, maple syrup is popular. It is made from the **sap** of maple trees. People use maple syrup on their pancakes at breakfast time.

It takes a lot of sap to make a small jar of maple syrup.

Shopping

People who live in big cities have many different places to shop. They can shop in large shopping malls or smaller corner stores.

In the West Edmonton Shopping Mall, people can view special **exhibits** and hundreds of different stores.

▼

Sometimes farmers travel to the nearest city to sell their produce.

◄

In small towns, people used to do much of their shopping by ordering things from catalogs. Now, **Internet shopping** is becoming more popular.

Houses and Homes

A large percentage of Candians live in cities. In cities, some Canadians rent apartments or houses. Other people own homes. Sometimes renting is cheaper than buying a house.

In Newfoundland, many homes are made of wood.

These modern-looking apartments are in Montreal.

There are many different types of houses in Canada. **Architects** design imaginative new apartments, too.

21

At Work

Luxury cars are built in this Canadian factory.

Most people in Canada work in cities. Some have jobs in factories. Towns have spread into farmland, making farming less common.

Some Canadians start
their own businesses.
Many people use
computers in offices or
in their homes.

Working from
home is popular.

23

Having Fun

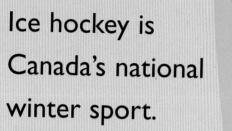

Ice hockey is Canada's national winter sport.

During the winter, Canadians participate in sports such as skiing, ice skating, and **tobogganing**. Many play and watch ice hockey as well.

In Canada, boating is popular because there are so many large lakes.

When the weather is warm, people often spend time at amusement parks or beaches. Some children spend their vacations at summer camps in the country.

Festivals

The Caribana Festival is held in Toronto every year.

Every year, different **festivals** are held all over Canada. Some of these include a comedy festival in Montreal and a children's film festival in Toronto.

Canadians often celebrate Canada Day with fireworks.

Canadians celebrate Victoria Day in May and Canada Day on July 1st. On these holidays, people might have a picnic or barbecue. At night, there are firework displays.

27

Canadian Scrapbook

This is a scrapbook of some everyday things you might find in Canada.

A badge from the Royal Ontario Museum.

A postcard of the CN (Canadian National) Tower in Toronto.

Canadians use Canadian dollars and cents. There are one hundred cents in a dollar.

Canadian travel tickets.

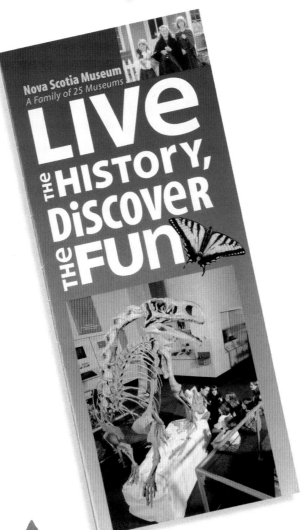

A pamphlet from a museum in Eastern Canada.

An entry ticket allowing one person to go up the CN Tower.

Glossary

Architect A person who draws up plans for a new building and then oversees its building.

Canola A plant used to make oil.

Exhibit A special display or piece of art.

Festival A time of celebration.

Internet shopping When people purchase items using a computer.

Official languages The language used in a country's official documents.

Prairie A large area of flat ground.

Public transportation A system of transportation, including buses and trains, that is available for everyone to use.

Range A row of mountains or hills.

Sap The sweet juice found inside a plant or tree. Sap is used to make syrup.

Tobogganing A sport where people slide over snow on a light sled that has runners.

Further Information

Some Canadian Words

anglophone	someone who speaks mainly English
click	a kilometer
francophone	someone who speaks mainly French
petrol	gasoline
poutine	chips covered in cheese and gravy
runners	tennis shoes
touque	knitted woolen cap
washroom	restroom
zed	the letter *z*

Further Reading From McGraw-Hill Children's Publishing

What's It Like to Live in Italy? (ISBN 1-57768-876-7)

What's It Like to Live in France? (ISBN 1-57768-875-9)

What's It Like to Live in Jamaica? (ISBN 1-57768-877-5)

Index

airplanes 12
amusement parks 25
apartments 20, 21

beaches 25
breakfast 17
bus 12, 13

Canadian Rocky
    Mountains 8
canola 15
cars 12, 13, 22
cable car 13
computers 23
crops 14

factories 22
farms 14, 19, 22
festivals 26, 27

forests 9

highways 12, 15

ice hockey 24
ice skating 24

lakes 25
languages 7

maple syrup 17
Montreal 6, 21, 26
mountains 8

Ottawa 4, 6

pancakes 17
picnics 16, 27
prairies 9, 14

restaurants 16

shopping malls 18
skiing 24
snowmobiles 13
sports 24
summer 10, 11, 25

tobogganing 24
Toronto 6, 26
trains 12, 13

Vancouver 6, 10

wheat 14
winter 4, 10, 11, 24